T0369117

Graced to Be
Chosen

Graced to Be Chosen

Inspirational Journal

Chosen Morris

GRACED TO BE CHOSEN
INSPIRATIONAL JOURNAL

iUniverse books may be ordered through booksellers or by contacting:

iUniverse
1663 Liberty Drive
Bloomington, IN 47403
www.iuniverse.com
1-800-Authors (1-800-288-4677)

ISBN: 978-1-4917-7042-9 (sc)
ISBN: 978-1-4917-7041-2 (e)

Library of Congress Control Number: 2015911081

Print information available on the last page.

iUniverse rev. date: 7/22/2015

Graced to Be

Preface

Hi, my name is Chosen Morris. Before I dive in to what could be considered an inspiring work journal for all to enjoy, I will quite simply say I have given you readers a few exercises to carry out in this book. I know that will have you not only prepared but ready for the next phase of your life by helping you to accomplish your goals, which you may have set on a back burner because of maybe a family obligation, feelings as if it were too late, or whatever other obstacles that have been in your way. With just a few easy steps at your very own pace, you'll be well on your way.

In Proverbs 13:19 (KJV), the Bible states, "A desired accomplished is sweet to the soul." Now we can all agree on that, whether we are a believer or not. Some things will still stand to be true, if applied.

As a motivated speaker, I have traveled across the globe, speaking and sharing insight of what I have experienced and learned to many different age groups and ethnic backgrounds, ranging from men and women, college students, working and staying-at-home moms, husbands and wives, single parents, and even religious and secular alike.

And in my findings with speaking to multiple individuals, I have come to learn that people are looking for simplicity and not the old, tired clichés they might have heard before. I'm not saying that the clichés are not fitting or working, but what I intend to explain is something new. I learned through experience that people desire want something new or even want to know how to work the clichés or sayings that they might have heard without going through a long, drawn-out period.

They're screaming phrases like, "Tell me simple words! I don't need to feel like I have to do so much work." And that's why I'm here for you--not to give you an unrealistic promise but to encourage you and give you a few simple steps where you can say, "Finally, someone understands me, Thank you."

I have been there, too. With the hustle and bustle, seeming like everyone wants it now and, truth be told, we all want it now. Who wants to wait? No one does. However, with these few simple steps I am inviting you to do with some daily inspirarational tips and encouragement, it will have you not only in control of setting realistic goals but becoming the master of positioning accurate objectives that will have you on your way to your very next achievement.

Get ready for the ride, readers, and thank you for allowing me to see you through your next.

Dare To Dream

Are you tired of hearing the same old clichés? Are you looking for something different? Or have you found yourself starting projects that you have yet to finish? You've just put them on the back burner and set them out for next time, but next time hasn't come yet. Or perhaps you're just not sure how to begin; however, you may feel that there has to be a much easier way to accomplish what might seem to be a difficult task or long process that everyone speaks of.

Well, get ready! Not only will this book give you the necessary steps to accomplish your goals and become masters of your own time to achieve your objectives at your very own pace, it is also designed to encourage and motivate you on a daily basis with inspirational quotes and scriptures for every day with your very own start-up that you can keep or share. Or maybe you can look back and just say, "This is where I finished."

But first, I would like to congratulate you. You have already accomplished a simple goal. It may not seem to be a big deal, but it is, and you achieved it by just picking up this book. Congratulations! You are on your way.

Let's Take a Look

On this page, I want you to write down five things that give you the most joy doing, your heart's desire, or just simply your dream. In Habakkuk 2:2, it tells us to write down our vision and seal it. So below, I have applied your "Graced to bes." Now all you have to do is finish writing it.

Tell me, what are you graced to be? What's your destiny? What would you like to achieve?

- Graced to be _____

- Graced to be _____

- Graced to be _____

- Graced to be _____

- Graced to be _____

Go for It

I consider this to be the most important part: applying a time limit to the goal you set out to accomplish your dream. So on this page; I would like you to place a realistic time limit to the goals that you have set.

- Time Goal: _____

- Time Goal: _____

- Time Goal: _____

- Time Goal: _____

- Time Goal: _____

Poem for You

Dear Dream,

Oh, how I despised and, at times, used to hate you with the many nos I got from you while on my quest to pursue you. Your rejection broke me. You taunted me with the success of Others While reminding me of my very own private failures and dreams I had yet to accomplish.

I ran when I heard you calling my name, struggling and fighting with my many disappointments and consistent let downs. After spending long hours in the dark with the many tears I shed, how will I ever feel so free to even pursue you again?

I believed in you. When you sent others to influence me, I made excuses and I ran from you. I was terrified of you. I read books about you. I saw all the rewards and accolades. I didn't want to dream again to what seemed to be a drizzling and far-fetched promise.

Then I woke up to that sweet, loving sound ringing, as if I attended a fulfilling seminar on a bay, and pleading with me that I try this dream again. I did. I dreamed again.

_____

_____

_____

_____

_____

_____

_____

_____

_____

_____

_____

_____

_____

_____

_____

Learn from the lessons your
pain has taught you.

_____

_____

_____

_____

_____

_____

_____

_____

_____

_____

_____

_____

Love yourself enough to let
go of what's hurting you.

_____

_____

_____

_____

_____

_____

_____

_____

_____

_____

_____

_____

_____

_____

_____

_____

_____

_____

Make a promise to commit to you.

_____

_____

_____

_____

_____

_____

_____

_____

_____

_____

_____

_____

_____

Wake up every day with
purpose and drive.

_____

_____

_____

_____

_____

_____

_____

_____

_____

_____

_____

_____

_____

_____

_____

_____

_____

The generous at heart will
be blessed *(Proverbs 22:9)*.

_____

_____

_____

_____

_____

_____

_____

_____

_____

_____

_____

_____

_____

_____

 Friendship abounds to them
with a pure heart and a
truthful lip. *(Proverbs 22:11)*.

_____

_____

_____

_____

_____

_____

_____

_____

_____

_____

_____

_____

_____

To the wise and youth hear me
and guard your heart *(Proverbs 23:19)*.

To whom who knows truth,
wisdom and instruction there's
no price *(Proverbs 23:23)*.

_____

_____

_____

_____

_____

_____

_____

_____

_____

_____

_____

_____

_____

_____

_____

There is hope for him who finds
wisdom and knowledge *(Proverbs 24:14)*.

_____

_____

_____

_____

_____

_____

_____

_____

_____

_____

_____

_____

_____

Even in preparation, there
will be challenges.

You don't have to be brave alone.

_____

_____

_____

_____

_____

_____

_____

_____

_____

_____

_____

_____

_____

_____

Help stop another generation
from dying internally.

_____

_____

_____

_____

_____

_____

_____

_____

_____

_____

_____

_____

_____

_____

_____

_____

_____

Create a peaceful world around you.

Don't quit in the middle of the battle.

_____

_____

_____

_____

_____

_____

_____

_____

_____

_____

_____

_____

_____

_____

It's unwise to judge those you
have yet come to know.

_____

_____

_____

_____

_____

_____

_____

_____

_____

_____

_____

_____

_____

_____

Appreciate life and the lives
of others around you.

_____

_____

_____

_____

_____

_____

_____

_____

_____

_____

_____

_____

_____

_____

_____

_____

_____

_____

Defeat comes to the Defeater.

Exercise your mind everyday
with positive thinking.

_____

_____

_____

_____

_____

_____

_____

_____

_____

_____

_____

_____

_____

_____

It's not the broken promises
that hurt; it's the expectations
behind the promise.

Don't wish for a better life, create a
better life by the choices you make.

_____

_____

_____

_____

_____

_____

_____

_____

_____

_____

_____

_____

_____

Dreams are made for those willing
to take the chance to go after them.

_____

_____

_____

_____

_____

_____

_____

_____

_____

_____

_____

_____

_____

_____

_____

A wise man will hear and increase
in his learning *(Proverbs 1:5)*.

_____

_____

_____

_____

_____

_____

_____

_____

_____

_____

_____

_____

_____

_____

_____

_____

Knowledge begins with
fearing the Lord *(Proverbs 1:7)*.

_____

_____

_____

_____

_____

_____

_____

_____

_____

_____

_____

_____

_____

Never feel compelled to doing
evil, but avoid it. *(Proverbs 1:10)*.

_____

_____

_____

_____

_____

_____

_____

_____

_____

_____

_____

_____

_____

Safety dwells in your
obedience *(Proverbs 1:33)*.

_____

_____

_____

_____

_____

_____

_____

_____

_____

_____

_____

_____

_____

Receive, incline, and discern with your heart; then you'll understand the fear of the Lord *(Proverbs 2:3-5)*.

Go beyond what you may
see because even what you
see has its limitations.

_____

_____

_____

_____

_____

_____

_____

_____

_____

_____

_____

_____

_____

_____

_____

Fear paralyzes your journey
while faith opens it.

He who gains insight gains
a better understanding.

Be known for what you
do, not who you are.

You'll appreciate the
fight when it's over.

31

_____

_____

_____

_____

_____

_____

_____

_____

_____

_____

_____

_____

_____

_____

_____

_____

A good word comes in due
season _(Proverbs. 15:23)._

_____

_____

_____

_____

_____

_____

_____

_____

_____

_____

_____

_____

_____

_____

_____

_____

He who walks with the wise will
be considered wise *(Proverbs 13:20)*.

_____

_____

_____

_____

_____

_____

_____

_____

_____

_____

_____

_____

_____

A happy heart is good for
your soul *(Proverbs 17:22)*.

_____

_____

_____

_____

_____

_____

_____

_____

_____

_____

_____

_____

_____

_____

_____

_____

_____

_____

# A foolish man grieves his father *(Proverbs 17:25)*.

_____

_____

_____

_____

_____

_____

_____

_____

_____

_____

_____

_____

_____

_____

A man of knowledge spares
his words *(Proverbs 17:27)*.

_____

_____

_____

_____

_____

_____

_____

_____

_____

_____

_____

_____

_____

_____

_____

_____

Better is he whom is known for what
he does than who he'll become.

_____

_____

_____

_____

_____

_____

_____

_____

_____

_____

_____

_____

_____

_____

Let God --- not man----dress you.

_____

_____

_____

_____

_____

_____

_____

_____

_____

_____

_____

_____

_____

_____

_____

_____

_____

Be great at being who
God called you to be.

_____

_____

_____

_____

_____

_____

_____

_____

_____

_____

_____

_____

Be your own duplicate
by being yourself.

Don't stop where you're at;
stop when you're done.

Do not be rebellious in spirit
and fear the Lord *(Proverbs 24:21)*.

_____

_____

_____

_____

_____

_____

_____

_____

_____

_____

_____

_____

_____

_____

_____

_____

Prepare yourself for your next
by working *(Proverbs. 24:27)*

_____

_____

_____

_____

_____

_____

_____

_____

_____

_____

_____

_____

_____

_____

_____

 A wise man will overlook an
offense and become slow
to anger *(Proverbs. 19:11)*.

_____

_____

_____

_____

_____

_____

_____

_____

_____

_____

_____

_____

_____

_____

_____

_____

  With patience, a calm spirit and soft speech will even to break the spirits of resistance *(Proverbs. 25:15)*.

The Lord is the light to our spirit,
who knows our hearts *(Proverbs. 20:27)*.

_____

_____

_____

_____

_____

_____

_____

_____

_____

_____

_____

_____

_____

_____

You can be your greatest defeat
or your strongest victory.

_____

_____

_____

_____

_____

_____

_____

_____

_____

_____

_____

_____

Opportunities are for those
who pursue them.

_____

_____

_____

_____

_____

_____

_____

_____

_____

_____

_____

_____

_____

_____

_____

_____

Don't just dream your
dream; become your dream
you're willing to see.

_____

_____

_____

_____

_____

_____

_____

_____

_____

_____

_____

_____

_____

_____

_____

Potential starts and ends with you.

_____

_____

_____

_____

_____

_____

_____

_____

_____

_____

_____

_____

_____

_____

_____

Soar off the failures that were
meant to break you.

_____

_____

_____

_____

_____

_____

_____

_____

_____

_____

_____

_____

_____

Let neither mercy or truths forsake
you, acknowledge God and He
will direct your path *(Proverbs. 3:3)*.

Only a fool will repeat the way
of his actions *(Proverbs. 26:11)*.

_____

_____

_____

_____

_____

_____

_____

_____

_____

_____

_____

_____

_____

_____

 Glorify the Lord God with all of your possessions', let Him be the first in your given and He'll return more unto you *(Proverbs. 3:9-10)*.

_____

_____

_____

_____

_____

_____

_____

_____

_____

_____

_____

_____

_____

_____

_____

To fear the Lord is not to consent
to evil of your own ways but
to depart from it *(Proverbs. 3:7)*.

_____

_____

_____

_____

_____

_____

_____

_____

_____

_____

_____

_____

_____

_____

Do not become angry with discipline
of the Lord, for whom the Lord
loves he corrects as a Mother and
Father to their Child *(Proverbs. 3:11-12)*.

_____

_____

_____

_____

_____

_____

_____

_____

_____

_____

_____

_____

_____

_____

_____

_____

_____

Compete with becoming a better
you then you were yesterday.

_____

_____

_____

_____

_____

_____

_____

_____

_____

_____

_____

_____

_____

_____

_____

To love is to win.

_____

_____

_____

_____

_____

_____

_____

_____

_____

_____

_____

_____

_____

_____

_____

Knowledge is the foundation to
understanding and the where
it is that you'll be going.

_____

_____

_____

_____

_____

_____

_____

_____

_____

_____

_____

_____

_____

God's goodness doesn't decrease
but yet increases in favor and stature.

_____

_____

_____

_____

_____

_____

_____

_____

_____

_____

_____

_____

_____

_____

Knowledge is obsolete for those who
don't know where they are going.

Keep sound wisdom and discretion and let it not depart from you. *(Proverbs. 3:21)*

_____

_____

_____

_____

_____

_____

_____

_____

_____

_____

_____

_____

_____

_____

Withhold no good deed from who
is honorable of it. *(Proverbs. 3:27)*.

Do not plan to do evil, against no one who lives accordingly *(Proverbs. 3:29)*.

_____

_____

_____

_____

_____

_____

_____

_____

_____

_____

_____

_____

_____

_____

_____

_____

Truthful words nourish many souls,
but a senseless man perishes
in his ways *(Proverbs. 10:21)*.

_____

_____

_____

_____

_____

_____

_____

_____

_____

_____

_____

_____

_____

_____

A good word to a depressed soul
makes one glad *(Proverbs. 12:25)*.

Let God's voice speak louder
than opinions of others.

_____

_____

_____

_____

_____

_____

_____

_____

_____

_____

_____

_____

_____

_____

_____

_____

Your greatest influencer
should be yourself.

Your best examination should
be self-examination.

_____

_____

_____

_____

_____

_____

_____

_____

_____

_____

_____

_____

Character is not only how you treat
others but how you treat yourself.

_____

_____

_____

_____

_____

_____

_____

_____

_____

_____

_____

_____

_____

_____

_____

_____

_____

You are love on display for all to see.

_____

_____

_____

_____

_____

_____

_____

_____

_____

_____

_____

_____

_____

_____

_____

_____

Operating in your gift opens doors for greater opportunities *(Proverbs. 18:16)*.

_____

_____

_____

_____

_____

_____

_____

_____

_____

_____

_____

_____

_____

_____

_____

_____

The way of your tongue promotes
life or death *(Proverbs: 18:21)*.

_____

_____

_____

_____

_____

_____

_____

_____

_____

_____

_____

_____

_____

  A man, who finds a good
wife, obtains favor from
the Lord *(Proverbs. 18:22)*.

_____

_____

_____

_____

_____

_____

_____

_____

_____

_____

_____

_____

_____

_____

To have a friend one must considered
himself friendly *(Proverbs. 18:24)*.

_____

_____

_____

_____

_____

_____

_____

_____

_____

_____

_____

_____

_____

_____

_____

_____

A thoughtful wife is from the Lord _(Proverbs 19:14)._

_____

_____

_____

_____

_____

_____

_____

_____

_____

_____

_____

_____

_____

_____

_____

_____

_____

_____

Let your silence speak louder for you.

_____

_____

_____

_____

_____

_____

_____

_____

_____

_____

_____

_____

_____

_____

When finding yourself, your world
opens up into knowing yourself.

With every trial comes a lesson.

Winning starts within.

To overcome your fear
is not to fear at all.

_____

_____

_____

_____

_____

_____

_____

_____

_____

_____

_____

_____

_____

_____

An unwise man has no delight
in understanding _(Proverbs.18:2)_.

_____

_____

_____

_____

_____

_____

_____

_____

_____

_____

_____

_____

_____

_____

_____

_____

Whosoever runs to the name of
the Lord will be safe *(Proverbs. 18:10)*.

_____

_____

_____

_____

_____

_____

_____

_____

_____

_____

_____

_____

_____

_____

Don't be an unwise person who
answers before he hears *(Proverbs. 18:13)*.

_____

_____

_____

_____

_____

_____

_____

_____

_____

_____

_____

_____

_____

_____

The heart of the wise obtains
knowledge *(Proverbs. 18.15)*.

_____

_____

_____

_____

_____

_____

_____

_____

_____

_____

_____

_____

_____

_____

You will be kept in
understanding *(Proverbs. 2:11)*.

_____

_____

_____

_____

_____

_____

_____

_____

_____

_____

_____

_____

_____

_____

You had purpose way before
others had their opinions.

_____

_____

_____

_____

_____

_____

_____

_____

_____

_____

_____

_____

_____

_____

False expectations create
false realities.

Your new life begins when
your old one ends.

To know is not knowing at all
to whom that thinks he knows
but yet knows nothing at all.

If you want to become
different, attract different.

_____

_____

_____

_____

_____

_____

_____

_____

_____

_____

_____

_____

_____

_____

_____

Luxury is not fitting for the
unwise *(Proverbs. 19:10)*.

_____

_____

_____

_____

_____

_____

_____

_____

_____

_____

_____

_____

_____

_____

_____

The way of the lord preserves
knowledge and keeps it *(Proverbs. 22 :12)*.

_____

_____

_____

_____

_____

_____

_____

_____

_____

_____

_____

_____

_____

_____

_____

_____

**It is not wise for one to overwork
to become rich** *(Proverbs. 23:4)*.

For as you think of yourself
so shall you be *(Proverbs 23:7)*

_____

_____

_____

_____

_____

_____

_____

_____

_____

_____

_____

_____

_____

_____

_____

_____

It is not good to withhold correction from a child *(Proverbs.23:13)*.

_____

_____

_____

_____

_____

_____

_____

_____

_____

_____

_____

_____

_____

_____

_____

There is conflict in hate, but in love
there's compassion *(Proverbs. 10:12)*.

Be of an understanding
heart *(Proverbs. 8:5)*.

_____

_____

_____

_____

_____

_____

_____

_____

_____

_____

_____

_____

_____

_____

_____

_____

_____

Favor comes to those who
pursue good *(Proverbs. 11:27)*.

_____

_____

_____

_____

_____

_____

_____

_____

_____

_____

_____

_____

_____

_____

_____

  When trials come and the pressure
start to unfold, stay planted in
the Lord, and He'll save you.

There's safety in the name Jesus.

Be a rebel for Christ.

_____

_____

_____

_____

_____

_____

_____

_____

_____

_____

_____

_____

_____

_____

_____

_____

You weren't created to fail but
to conquer in opposition.

_____

_____

_____

_____

_____

_____

_____

_____

_____

_____

_____

_____

_____

 Strength wasn't created for the strongest in battle but for the one who endures to the end.

Happy is he who finds wisdom
and understandings *(Proverbs. 3:13)*.

_____

_____

_____

_____

_____

_____

_____

_____

_____

_____

_____

_____

_____

_____

_____

Keep watch over your heart, for out
of it flows gentleness' *(Proverbs. 4:26)*.

_____
_____
_____
_____
_____
_____
_____
_____
_____
_____
_____
_____
_____
_____
_____
_____

Take a considered thought in the
way you should go. *(Proverbs. 4:26).*

_____

_____

_____

_____

_____

_____

_____

_____

_____

_____

_____

_____

_____

_____

_____

_____

Keep the laws of my word,
secure them in your heart, for it'll
keep you in time *(Proverbs. 3:1)*.

Do not respond to a fool,
least you'll be considered
just as him *(Proverbs. 26:4)*.

_____

_____

_____

_____

_____

_____

_____

_____

_____

_____

_____

_____

_____

_____

Never allow your past to determine
the outcome of your future.

_____

_____

_____

_____

_____

_____

_____

_____

_____

_____

_____

_____

_____

_____

Regret comes when we don't take
the chances we should have taken.

_____

_____

_____

_____

_____

_____

_____

_____

_____

_____

_____

_____

_____

_____

Knowledge is acquired
through experience.

_____

_____

_____

_____

_____

_____

_____

_____

_____

_____

_____

_____

_____

_____

_____

_____

Free yourself from the
opinions of others.

_____

_____

_____

_____

_____

_____

_____

_____

_____

_____

_____

_____

_____

The best sacrifice is self-sacrifice.

Nothing compares to
wisdom *(Proverbs. 8:11)*.

_____

_____

_____

_____

_____

_____

_____

_____

_____

_____

_____

_____

_____

_____

_____

_____

Do not forsake instructions
when given *(Proverbs. 8:33)*.

Forsake foolish behavior
and live *(Proverbs.9:6)*.

_____

_____

_____

_____

_____

_____

_____

_____

_____

_____

_____

_____

_____

_____

_____

_____

An obnoxious women knows
nothing *(Proverbs. 9:13)*.

_____

_____

_____

_____

_____

_____

_____

_____

_____

_____

_____

_____

_____

_____

_____

The hand of the diligent makes one rich *(Proverbs 10:4)*.

_____

_____

_____

_____

_____

_____

_____

_____

_____

_____

_____

_____

Never despise small begging's.

There's freedom in being you.

121

_____

_____

_____

_____

_____

_____

_____

_____

_____

_____

_____

_____

_____

_____

Become the legacy you
want the world to see.

Change starts and begins with you.

_____

_____

_____

_____

_____

_____

_____

_____

_____

_____

_____

_____

_____

 Forgiveness is a process, but
the characteristics of love will
produce the outcome.

_____

_____

_____

_____

_____

_____

_____

_____

_____

_____

_____

_____

_____

_____

A preserved life is for those who
guard their tongue *(Proverbs. 13:3)*.

_____

_____

_____

_____

_____

_____

_____

_____

_____

_____

_____

_____

_____

_____

A desire accomplished is sweet
to the soul *(Proverbs. 13:19)*.

Wisdom is found to whom who
has understanding *(Proverbs. 10:13)*.

_____

_____

_____

_____

_____

_____

_____

_____

_____

_____

_____

_____

_____

_____

When the lord blesses you
with riches it comes with
no sorrow *(Proverbs. 10:22)*.

_____

_____

_____

_____

_____

_____

_____

_____

_____

_____

_____

_____

_____

_____

_____

_____

Favor comes with
understanding *(Proverbs. 13:15)*.

_____

_____

_____

_____

_____

_____

_____

_____

_____

_____

_____

_____

_____

An opinionated person has
nothing but an opinion.

Happiness starts with you first.

With authenticity comes
appreciation.

Stand in integrity even if it
means you're standing alone.

_____

_____

_____

_____

_____

_____

_____

_____

_____

_____

_____

_____

_____

Positive thinking creates
positive outcomes.

_____

_____

_____

_____

_____

_____

_____

_____

_____

_____

_____

_____

_____

Fearing the Lord will prolong
your days *(Proverbs. 10:27)*.

A knowledgeable man will act in discretion *(Proverbs. 13:16)*.

_____

_____

_____

_____

_____

_____

_____

_____

_____

_____

_____

_____

_____

 There's nothing found in pride,
but to whom who seeks advice
there's wisdom *(Proverbs. 13:10)*.

_____

_____

_____

_____

_____

_____

_____

_____

_____

_____

_____

_____

_____

_____

**Favor is found with good
judgement** *(Proverbs. 13:15)*.

_____

_____

_____

_____

_____

_____

_____

_____

_____

_____

_____

_____

_____

_____

_____

_____

Let not the words of my mouth
forsake you *(Proverbs. 5:7)*.

_____

_____

_____

_____

_____

_____

_____

_____

_____

_____

_____

_____

_____

_____

_____

Your only bond by the limitations
you set for yourself.

_____

_____

_____

_____

_____

_____

_____

_____

_____

_____

_____

_____

_____

_____

_____

_____

_____

 With every barrier comes potential
that you refuse to face.

_____

_____

_____

_____

_____

_____

_____

_____

_____

_____

_____

_____

_____

Replace fear with the
motion to become.

Separations are required on
different levels of purpose.

_____

_____

_____

_____

_____

_____

_____

_____

_____

_____

_____

_____

_____

 You must apply an amount of
courage in order to continue
what you started.

_____

_____

_____

_____

_____

_____

_____

_____

_____

_____

_____

_____

_____

_____

 There are repercussions with the words you speak. *(Proverbs. 6:2)*.

An Adulterous has lack of
understanding *(Proverbs. 6:32)*.

_____

_____

_____

_____

_____

_____

_____

_____

_____

_____

_____

_____

_____

_____

_____

_____

The lord kept you from the
beginning of time *(Proverbs. 8:22)*.

_____

_____

_____

_____

_____

_____

_____

_____

_____

_____

_____

_____

_____

Whosoever finds the Lord comes
into life and favor *(Proverbs. 8:32).*

There is a blessing for he who
doeth what is right *(Proverbs. 10:6)*.

_____

_____

_____

_____

_____

_____

_____

_____

_____

_____

_____

_____

Define your story; don't allow
your story to define you.

You cannot think out of the box
if you're never limited to one.

_____

_____

_____

_____

_____

_____

_____

_____

_____

_____

_____

_____

Break the mole of being
you by becoming who
you're designed to be.

Be cautious on being the cause
of breaking up a happy home.

_____

_____

_____

_____

_____

_____

_____

_____

_____

_____

_____

_____

Don't miss what God is trying to say
by the distractions of your yesterday.

_____

_____

_____

_____

_____

_____

_____

_____

_____

_____

_____

_____

_____

_____

_____

_____

To whom who walks in integrity
securely will follow him *(Proverbs. 10:9)*.

_____

_____

_____

_____

_____

_____

_____

_____

_____

_____

_____

_____

_____

_____

_____

_____

Hold your peace *(Proverbs. 11:12)*.

_____

_____

_____

_____

_____

_____

_____

_____

_____

_____

_____

_____

_____

_____

There is quality in living a
righteous life *(Proverbs. 11:19)*.

_____

_____

_____

_____

_____

_____

_____

_____

_____

_____

_____

_____

The wise loves knowledge
and instruction. *(Proverbs. 12:1).*

_____

_____

_____

_____

_____

_____

_____

_____

_____

_____

_____

_____

_____

_____

_____

_____

_____

 The Lord favors a good
man *(Proverbs. 12:2)*.

_____

_____

_____

_____

_____

_____

_____

_____

_____

_____

_____

_____

_____

_____

_____

_____

Success is not determined by
what you have but by merely
who you'll become.

_____

_____

_____

_____

_____

_____

_____

_____

_____

_____

_____

_____

_____

_____

_____

Success is free to those
who go after it.

Believing with uncertainty
is not believing at all.

You are the product of the
actions that you chose.

_____

_____

_____

_____

_____

_____

_____

_____

_____

_____

_____

_____

_____

How you think creates your world.

The tongue of the righteous man stands in truth *(Proverbs. 12:17)*.

Choose your friends
carefully *(Proverbs. 12:26)*

You'll find nothing in being lazy, but to whom who works diligently wealth *(Proverbs. 13:4)*.

_____

_____

_____

_____

_____

_____

_____

_____

_____

_____

_____

_____

Laughter is found in the heart
of a fool to whom who thinks
sin is funny *(Proverbs. 14:9)*.

_____

_____

_____

_____

_____

_____

_____

_____

_____

_____

_____

_____

_____

Wealth gained in dishonesty
will not last *(Proverbs. 13:11)*.

_____

_____

_____

_____

_____

_____

_____

_____

_____

_____

_____

_____

_____

_____

It's not your outer but more of your
inner struggle that is killing you.

The character of your deeds
will vindicate your wisdom.

_____

_____

_____

_____

_____

_____

_____

_____

_____

_____

_____

_____

_____

_____

In every gifting, there
will be a struggle.

_____

_____

_____

_____

_____

_____

_____

_____

_____

_____

_____

_____

_____

_____

_____

Victory is in the process
of your waiting.

_____

_____

_____

_____

_____

_____

_____

_____

_____

_____

_____

_____

_____

_____

Life will live for you if
you don't live it.

A wise man will leave an inheritance to his children's children. *(Proverbs. 13:22)*

A man with discretion will act
accordingly *(Proverbs. 13:16)*

_____

_____

_____

_____

_____

_____

_____

_____

_____

_____

_____

_____

_____

_____

_____

_____

If a man speaks having no knowledge
leave his presence *(Proverbs. 14:7)*

_____

_____

_____

_____

_____

_____

_____

_____

_____

_____

_____

_____

_____

Even in laughter in the heart
may sorrow (*Proverbs. 14:13*).

_____

_____

_____

_____

_____

_____

_____

_____

_____

_____

_____

_____

_____

_____

_____

_____

A deceitful man will speak
lies *(Proverbs. 14:25)*.

_____

_____

_____

_____

_____

_____

_____

_____

_____

_____

_____

_____

Words are voided with
no action applied.

_____

_____

_____

_____

_____

_____

_____

_____

_____

_____

_____

_____

_____

_____

_____

_____

Your greatest potential is in what
you have yet to reach for.

_____

_____

_____

_____

_____

_____

_____

_____

_____

_____

_____

_____

_____

_____

Your yesterday is not as merely
as important as your today.

_____

_____

_____

_____

_____

_____

_____

_____

_____

_____

_____

_____

_____

_____

_____

Your hardest confrontation is
the ones you want face.

_____

_____

_____

_____

_____

_____

_____

_____

_____

_____

_____

_____

Nothing comes to a
sleeper but a dream.

_____

_____

_____

_____

_____

_____

_____

_____

_____

_____

_____

_____

_____

_____

_____

_____

 Acting in impulse is foolish, but to who that is slowly angered there lies understanding *(Proverbs. 14:29)*.

_____

_____

_____

_____

_____

_____

_____

_____

_____

_____

_____

_____

_____

_____

_____

There is life in him who has a happy heart, but in whom who is envious darkness *(Proverbs. 14:30)*.

_____

_____

_____

_____

_____

_____

_____

_____

_____

_____

_____

_____

_____

_____

The heart of a righteous man
studies how to answer, while the
unwise does not *(Proverbs. 15:28)*.

_____

_____

_____

_____

_____

_____

_____

_____

_____

_____

_____

_____

_____

Better is he who has little then has much with trouble *(Proverbs. 15:16)*.

_____

_____

_____

_____

_____

_____

_____

_____

_____

_____

_____

_____

_____

Troubled comes to those who
is greedy for gain _(Proverbs. 15:27)_

_____

_____

_____

_____

_____

_____

_____

_____

_____

_____

_____

_____

_____

Know where you're at so you'll
know where you're going.

Celebrate your winnings at your best.

_____

_____

_____

_____

_____

_____

_____

_____

_____

_____

_____

_____

_____

For every theory lies logic
and, with logic, reality.

_____

_____

_____

_____

_____

_____

_____

_____

_____

_____

_____

_____

_____

Prepare for your now today.

_____

_____

_____

_____

_____

_____

_____

_____

_____

_____

_____

_____

_____

_____

You're only as good as the
yesterday you created today.

When the righteousness of
your ways please the Lord,
even to your enemies will make
peace with you (*Proverbs. 16:7*).

_____

_____

_____

_____

_____

_____

_____

_____

_____

_____

_____

_____

_____

_____

The Lord is disdained with whom who has prideful heart *(Proverbs. 16:5).*

_____

_____

_____

_____

_____

_____

_____

_____

_____

_____

_____

_____

_____

_____

A man plans out his way but the Lord directs the steps. *(Proverbs. 16:9)*.

Be of a humble and kind
spirit *(Proverbs. 16:19)*.

With pride comes
destruction *(Proverbs. 16:18)*.

You're the results of your thinking.

Self-denial is your worst denial.

_____

_____

_____

_____

_____

_____

_____

_____

_____

_____

_____

_____

_____

_____

What you give power to controls you.

To be absolutely certain of a
thing is not being certain at all.

_____

_____

_____

_____

_____

_____

_____

_____

_____

_____

_____

_____

_____

_____

_____

Time wasted is life wasted.

Happy is he who trusts in
the Lord *(Proverbs. 17:3)*.

The Lord tests the heart *(Proverbs 17:3)*.

_____

_____

_____

_____

_____

_____

_____

_____

_____

_____

_____

_____

_____

_____

_____

_____

Rebuking a wise man is more
effective than to rebuke
a fool *(Proverbs 17:10)*.

_____

_____

_____

_____

_____

_____

_____

_____

_____

_____

_____

_____

_____

_____

_____

Stop a disagreement before
it starts *(Proverbs 17:14)*.

The Lord knows every
decision *(Proverbs 16:33)*.

_____

_____

_____

_____

_____

_____

_____

_____

_____

_____

_____

_____

_____

_____

_____

_____

You choose the life you
want to live by living the life
that you choose to live.

_____

_____

_____

_____

_____

_____

_____

_____

_____

_____

_____

_____

_____

_____

_____

 An unaccomplished dream is
an unaccomplished goal.

Build from the rocks that
were thrown at you.

The way you treat others
characterizes you.

_____

_____

_____

_____

_____

_____

_____

_____

_____

_____

_____

_____

_____

_____

_____

_____

God is already in your yesterday
as well as your today.

A good friend loves at all
times *(Proverbs 17:17)*.

_____

_____

_____

_____

_____

_____

_____

_____

_____

_____

_____

_____

_____

_____

There is no pleasure found in condemning the right, And justifying that which is wrong *(Proverbs 17: 15)*.

_____

_____

_____

_____

_____

_____

_____

_____

_____

_____

_____

_____

_____

_____

Better is he who is slow
to anger *(Proverbs 16:32)*.

_____

_____

_____

_____

_____

_____

_____

_____

_____

_____

_____

_____

_____

_____

Wisdom is found in a man of
understanding *(Proverbs 14:33)*.

_____

_____

_____

_____

_____

_____

_____

_____

_____

_____

_____

_____

_____

Even a child knows what is
right from wrong *(Proverbs 20:3)*.

Sustained knowledge is
your greatest revenue.

_____

_____

_____

_____

_____

_____

_____

_____

_____

_____

_____

_____

_____

_____

_____

 Unlocked potential creates
an unlocked path.

_____

_____

_____

_____

_____

_____

_____

_____

_____

_____

_____

_____

_____

Just because it hasn't happened yet
doesn't mean it want happen at all.

_____

_____

_____

_____

_____

_____

_____

_____

_____

_____

_____

_____

_____

_____

_____

_____

Fruit is only produced off
a message received.

Your greatest begging's are
the ones you can't see.

_____

_____

_____

_____

_____

_____

_____

_____

_____

_____

_____

_____

_____

_____

_____

Do not repay those who have wronged you wait on the Lord and He will save you *(Proverbs 20:22)*.

_____

_____

_____

_____

_____

_____

_____

_____

_____

_____

_____

_____

_____

_____

_____

_____

For one to be wise must first be wise for thy self *(Proverbs 9:12)*.

_____

_____

_____

_____

_____

_____

_____

_____

_____

_____

_____

_____

_____

_____

_____

_____

A wise person will sustain all
knowledge _(Proverbs 10:14)_.

_____

_____

_____

_____

_____

_____

_____

_____

_____

_____

_____

_____

_____

_____

_____

The hatred at heart has lying lips. And he who spreads lies is a fool *(Proverbs 10:18)*.

_____

_____

_____

_____

_____

_____

_____

_____

_____

_____

_____

_____

_____

_____

_____

_____

_____

A fool dies from lack of wisdom. _(Proverbs 10:21)._

Success is not handed but captured.

Feed your soul with the
knowledge of today.

Live in hopes of a greater tomorrow.

_____

_____

_____

_____

_____

_____

_____

_____

_____

_____

_____

_____

_____

_____

It's not merely what you
receive but what you give.

_____

_____

_____

_____

_____

_____

_____

_____

_____

_____

_____

_____

_____

Your fight is not about your
yesterday, but your today.

The expectations of the wicked
man will perish. *(Proverbs 10:28)*

_____

_____

_____

_____

_____

_____

_____

_____

_____

_____

_____

_____

_____

_____

There is strength found in him
who lives right *(Proverbs 10:29)*.

_____

_____

_____

_____

_____

_____

_____

_____

_____

_____

_____

_____

_____

_____

_____

_____

There's wisdom in being humble
and in pride shame. *(Proverbs 11:2)*

_____

_____

_____

_____

_____

_____

_____

_____

_____

_____

_____

_____

_____

_____

The righteous man will be delivered
from their troubles *(Proverbs 11:8)*

_____

_____

_____

_____

_____

_____

_____

_____

_____

_____

_____

_____

_____

_____

_____

_____

_____

_____

A envious man who despises others
no wisdom is found *(Proverbs 11:12)*

_____

_____

_____

_____

_____

_____

_____

_____

_____

_____

_____

_____

_____

Don't cheat yourself out
of opportunities you're
unwilling to take.

_____

_____

_____

_____

_____

_____

_____

_____

_____

_____

_____

_____

_____

_____

_____

You're greater than your yesterday.

Position yourself for your next level.

The success you feed will be
the success that grows.

_____

_____

_____

_____

_____

_____

_____

_____

_____

_____

_____

_____

_____

Don't die a copy when you
were created a novelty.

_____

_____

_____

_____

_____

_____

_____

_____

_____

_____

_____

_____

_____

_____

_____

_____

_____

Honor is bestowed on a woman
with a gracious spirit *(Proverbs 11:16)*

_____

_____

_____

_____

_____

_____

_____

_____

_____

_____

_____

_____

_____

_____

Trouble comes to those with
cruel intentions, but to whom of
good deeds honor. *(Proverbs 11:17)*

You'll find good in desiring
what is right *(Proverbs 11:23)*

_____

_____

_____

_____

_____

_____

_____

_____

_____

_____

_____

_____

_____

Favor is found in him to whom who goes after what is good. *(Proverbs 11:27)*

It is unwise for a man to trust in
his own riches. *(Proverbs 11:28)*

_____

_____

_____

_____

_____

_____

_____

_____

_____

_____

_____

_____

_____

_____

Get up; stay up; be positive.

To love without loving
is not loving at all.

_____

_____

_____

_____

_____

_____

_____

_____

_____

_____

_____

_____

_____

Self- distraction is your
worse distraction.

Every situation has a solution, as
every prospect has a future.

_____

_____

_____

_____

_____

_____

_____

_____

_____

_____

_____

_____

You'll find no happiness
in being the victim.

_____

_____

_____

_____

_____

_____

_____

_____

_____

_____

_____

_____

_____

_____

_____

_____

It's stupid to hate correction. *(Proverbs 12:1)*

_____

_____

_____

_____

_____

_____

_____

_____

_____

_____

_____

_____

_____

A sagacious woman is the crown
of her husband. *(Proverbs 12:4)*

It is wise to whom who seek wise counsel, but to be right in your own eyes is foolish. *(Proverbs 12:15)*

_____

_____

_____

_____

_____

_____

_____

_____

_____

_____

_____

_____

_____

_____

_____

 A man of a deceitful heart finds delight in doing what's evil. But, a good man peace and joy. *(Proverbs 12:20)*

Better is a home with little contention than a home full of strife. *(Proverbs 17:1)*

_____

_____

_____

_____

_____

_____

_____

_____

_____

_____

_____

_____

To understand life is one thing
but to live it is another.

You cannot go to a place where
you're afraid to take a step to go.

_____

_____

_____

_____

_____

_____

_____

_____

_____

_____

_____

_____

_____

_____

_____

Success is not by design;
rather, intentional.

_____

_____

_____

_____

_____

_____

_____

_____

_____

_____

_____

_____

_____

You cannot live your life if
your too busy trying to live
your neighbor's life.

Never neglect your
dreams for a fantasy.

_____

_____

_____

_____

_____

_____

_____

_____

_____

_____

_____

_____

_____

_____

_____

Evildoers take pleasure in lying
lips, and gives heed to the
gossiping tongue. *(Proverbs 17:4)*

_____

_____

_____

_____

_____

_____

_____

_____

_____

_____

_____

_____

An unwise man knows nothing
of excellent speech. *(Proverbs 17:7)*

An evil man is rebellious in
all his ways. *(Proverbs 17:10)*

_____

_____

_____

_____

_____

_____

_____

_____

_____

_____

_____

_____

_____

_____

No good is found in those with
a deceitful heart. *(Proverbs 17:20)*

An evil man accepts bribes
for doing evil. *(Proverbs 17:23)*

_____

_____

_____

_____

_____

_____

_____

_____

_____

_____

_____

_____

_____

Don't be the creator of
your own misery.

Embrace your difference.

_____

_____

_____

_____

_____

_____

_____

_____

_____

_____

_____

_____

_____

_____

_____

  The only box you have to think outside of is the limitations you have placed on your thinking.

_____

_____

_____

_____

_____

_____

_____

_____

_____

_____

_____

_____

_____

_____

_____

_____

You can't think outside of the box
if there is no box to think out of.

Never allow anyone to devalue you.

Be genuine in all things you do.

_____

_____

_____

_____

_____

_____

_____

_____

_____

_____

_____

_____

_____

_____

_____

 Be thankful for each given day.

_____

_____

_____

_____

_____

_____

_____

_____

_____

_____

_____

_____

_____

_____

_____

_____

It's hard to gain trust from which
judgement was cast on *(Proverbs 18:19)*

_____

_____

_____

_____

_____

_____

_____

_____

_____

_____

_____

_____

_____

_____

_____

A man of discretion will be
slow to anger. *(Proverbs 19:11)*

_____

_____

_____

_____

_____

_____

_____

_____

_____

_____

_____

_____

_____

_____

_____

A lazy man suffers from
hunger *(Proverbs 19:11)*.

_____

_____

_____

_____

_____

_____

_____

_____

_____

_____

_____

_____

_____

_____

_____

_____

 Care for your child while there's still
hope in him and do not set your
heart on their destruction *(Proverbs 19:18)*

Have pity on the poor *(Proverbs 19:17)*.

_____

_____

_____

_____

_____

_____

_____

_____

_____

_____

_____

_____

_____

_____

Move past the troubles of your
yesterday and focus on the
begging's of your today.

_____

_____

_____

_____

_____

_____

_____

_____

_____

_____

_____

_____

_____

_____

Sign off on the things
you can not control.

_____

_____

_____

_____

_____

_____

_____

_____

_____

_____

_____

_____

_____

_____

_____

_____

_____

Your only control is
how you respond.

_____

_____

_____

_____

_____

_____

_____

_____

_____

_____

_____

_____

_____

_____

_____

Be mindful of the things you say.

_____

_____

_____

_____

_____

_____

_____

_____

_____

_____

_____

_____

_____

Live selflessly.

_____

_____

_____

_____

_____

_____

_____

_____

_____

_____

_____

_____

_____

_____

Receive instructions now so you can avoid foolishness later *(Proverbs 19:20)*

_____

_____

_____

_____

_____

_____

_____

_____

_____

_____

_____

_____

_____

_____

Those who are rebuked
in understanding discerns
knowledge *(Proverbs 19:25)*

Who can vouch for those
who proclaim of their own
goodness? *(Proverbs 20:6)*

_____

_____

_____

_____

_____

_____

_____

_____

_____

_____

_____

_____

_____

_____

Blessings will be found on your
children for those who stand
in their integrity *(Proverbs 20:7)*

_____

_____

_____

_____

_____

_____

_____

_____

_____

_____

_____

_____

_____

_____

_____

_____

Appreciate those who
appreciate you.

_____

_____

_____

_____

_____

_____

_____

_____

_____

_____

_____

_____

_____

_____

There is gratitude in appreciating.

_____

_____

_____

_____

_____

_____

_____

_____

_____

_____

_____

_____

_____

_____

_____

_____

 Don't live your life doing what
you weren't called to do.

_____

_____

_____

_____

_____

_____

_____

_____

_____

_____

_____

_____

_____

_____

God knows the ending of your story.

_____

_____

_____

_____

_____

_____

_____

_____

_____

_____

_____

_____

_____

_____

_____

_____

Do more complain less.

_____

_____

_____

_____

_____

_____

_____

_____

_____

_____

_____

_____

_____

_____

_____

_____

See yourself as God sees you.

It is unwise to punish those
who are right *(Proverbs 17:26)*

_____

_____

_____

_____

_____

_____

_____

_____

_____

_____

_____

_____

_____

_____

Even a fool will be counted wise
when he hold his tongue. *(Proverbs 17:28)*

_____

_____

_____

_____

_____

_____

_____

_____

_____

_____

_____

_____

_____

_____

Isolation will soon lead to
ideal desires *(Proverbs 18:1)*

_____

_____

_____

_____

_____

_____

_____

_____

_____

_____

_____

_____

_____

An angry man has no desire in understanding, but expressing their own wrath. *(Proverbs 18:2)*

Contention is found on the
lips of a fool *(Proverbs 18:6)*

_____

_____

_____

_____

_____

_____

_____

_____

_____

_____

_____

_____

_____

_____

_____

Your goal should line up
with your destiny.

Don't reach for the stars
reach for no limits.

_____

_____

_____

_____

_____

_____

_____

_____

_____

_____

_____

_____

_____

_____

_____

Your dream should be bigger
than what you can achieve.

_____

_____

_____

_____

_____

_____

_____

_____

_____

_____

_____

_____

_____

_____

_____

_____

Celebrate you.

_____

_____

_____

_____

_____

_____

_____

_____

_____

_____

_____

_____

_____

_____

There's no arrogance in
knowing your value.

Spend time with you.

_____

_____

_____

_____

_____

_____

_____

_____

_____

_____

_____

_____

_____

Value those around you.

_____

_____

_____

_____

_____

_____

_____

_____

_____

_____

_____

_____

_____

_____

_____

_____

Do something kind for someone
other than yourself.

It's okay to cry, but when you're
done, light a candle and shine.

Keep smiling even when
it hurts to do so.

_____

_____

_____

_____

_____

_____

_____

_____

_____

_____

_____

_____

_____

_____

An unwise tongue is of your
own destruction *(Proverbs 18:7)*

_____

_____

_____

_____

_____

_____

_____

_____

_____

_____

_____

_____

_____

_____

_____

_____

Destruction is before a man
with no humility *(Proverbs 18:12)*

_____

_____

_____

_____

_____

_____

_____

_____

_____

_____

_____

_____

_____

_____

_____

_____

 Shame on him who answers
before he hears *(Proverbs 18:13)*

In the times of your brokenness the spirit will keep you. *(Proverbs 18:14)*

Contention is caused when
judgement is cast *(Proverbs 18:18)*

Don't become what you
don't want to see.

_____

_____

_____

_____

_____

_____

_____

_____

_____

_____

_____

_____

_____

_____

Celebrate one victory at a time.

Poverty will come to the
sleeper *(Proverbs 20:13)*

_____

_____

_____

_____

_____

_____

_____

_____

_____

_____

_____

_____

_____

_____

_____

_____

Disassociate yourself with those
who are taken by the flattering
of a deceitful lip. *(Proverbs 20:25)*

_____

_____

_____

_____

_____

_____

_____

_____

_____

_____

_____

_____

_____

_____

_____

_____

_____

It is unwise for a man to reconsider a vow made to him holy *(Proverbs 20:25)*

_____

_____

_____

_____

_____

_____

_____

_____

_____

_____

_____

_____

_____

_____

_____

Glory and strength is in youth, and
the old grey hair. *(Proverbs 20:29)*

A man who works with diligence
will have plenty. *(Proverbs 21:5)*

_____

_____

_____

_____

_____

_____

_____

_____

_____

_____

_____

_____

_____

You're a champion

_____

_____

_____

_____

_____

_____

_____

_____

_____

_____

_____

_____

_____

_____

_____

_____

Winning comes to the one who
sees himself or herself winning.

You can't win a fight focusing
on your opponent.

Don't cheat yourself by living
below your potential.

_____

_____

_____

_____

_____

_____

_____

_____

_____

_____

_____

_____

_____

_____

_____

No favor will be found for anyone
who desires to do evil. *(Proverbs 21:10)*

_____

_____

_____

_____

_____

_____

_____

_____

_____

_____

_____

_____

_____

_____

_____

_____

A bribe given in secret
Causes anger *(Proverbs 21:14)*

_____

_____

_____

_____

_____

_____

_____

_____

_____

_____

_____

_____

_____

_____

_____

The Lord finds pleasure in
him who enjoys doing what
is right. *(Proverbs 21:15)*

He who enjoys the spoils of the rich
shall be made poor. *(Proverbs 21:17)*

_____

_____

_____

_____

_____

_____

_____

_____

_____

_____

_____

_____

_____

_____

_____

_____

A man of pride becomes arrogant at the mention of their name *(Proverbs 21:24)*

_____

_____

_____

_____

_____

_____

_____

_____

_____

_____

_____

_____

_____

_____

Take part of your day to silence it.

Appreciate the things you don't have.

Appreciation comes to the
things that don't come easily.

_____

_____

_____

_____

_____

_____

_____

_____

_____

_____

_____

_____

_____

_____

Pray each day and every day.

There's no age where
wisdom is found.

There is hope for them who find
wisdom and knowledge *(Proverbs 24:14)*

_____

_____

_____

_____

_____

_____

_____

_____

_____

_____

_____

_____

_____

_____

God takes the things you proclaim you did not know into consideration. *(Proverbs 24:12)*

_____

_____

_____

_____

_____

_____

_____

_____

_____

_____

_____

_____

_____

_____

_____

_____

A fearful man is slain by his
own ignorance. *(Proverbs 22:13)*

_____

_____

_____

_____

_____

_____

_____

_____

_____

_____

_____

_____

_____

_____

_____

  The heart of a child is foolish in his was but stern correction will cause it to cease. _(Proverbs 22:15)_

The wise have been taught to
answer in truth. *(Proverbs 22:21)*

It's unwise to put a color
on discrimination.

_____

_____

_____

_____

_____

_____

_____

_____

_____

_____

_____

_____

_____

_____

Don't close out the
heart of the youth.

It's not a failed system; it's more of failed leadership.

_____

_____

_____

_____

_____

_____

_____

_____

_____

_____

_____

_____

_____

Give your children the gift of
hearing and recognizing them.

Be your own creator of peace
by living peaceably.

_____

_____

_____

_____

_____

_____

_____

_____

_____

_____

_____

_____

_____

_____

Forsake the presence of an angry
man, and do not make friends
with him for he will be grievous
to your soul *(Proverbs 22:24)*

_____

_____

_____

_____

_____

_____

_____

_____

_____

_____

_____

_____

_____

_____

_____

_____

 Do not eat or drink with a deceitful man, for he says to you come but his heart is far from you. *(Proverbs 23:6-7)*

_____

_____

_____

_____

_____

_____

_____

_____

_____

_____

_____

_____

_____

_____

_____

The Lord rejoices with a wise
heart that speaks of rightful
things *(Proverbs 23: 15-16)*

Be diligent in the Lord and not envious of sinners and your hope will not be cut from you. *(Proverbs 23:17-18)*

A man of knowledge increases
in strength *(Proverbs 24:5)*

Pick someone up before
you tear them down.

_____

_____

_____

_____

_____

_____

_____

_____

_____

_____

_____

_____

Discern with your heart.

Don't get buried with your
unaccomplished dream.

_____

_____

_____

_____

_____

_____

_____

_____

_____

_____

_____

_____

Don't waste your life living the
dreams of others and having
yet to pursue your own.

_____

_____

_____

_____

_____

_____

_____

_____

_____

_____

_____

_____

_____

_____

_____

_____

_____

See Past Yourself.

Conclusion

Oftentimes in life, we as people make things way too complicated when we all are just looking for something realistic and simple rather than expectations that we set for ourselves or others. But something real that we can look forward to accomplishing. And in this book, that's what I aimed to give you my readers. And have you become masters of your own time and set realistic goals that will carry you to your next.

So I encourage my readers to continue applying yourselves and see what you are graced to be because we are all graced to be something bigger than us. Thank you for allowing me to help you to discover what you are graced to be. And don't beat yourself up if you don't accomplish the goal set for the time that you may have placed for yourself. Just make a new one and continue.